STEM IN FIGURE SKATING

SportsZone

An Imprint of Abdo Publishing
abdopublishing.com

BY MARNE VENTURA

ABDOPUBLISHING.COM

Published by Abdo Publishing, a division of ABDO, PO Box 398166, Minneapolis, Minnesota 55439. Copyright © 2018 by Abdo Consulting Group, Inc. International copyrights reserved in all countries. No part of this book may be reproduced in any form without written permission from the publisher. SportsZone™ is a trademark and logo of Abdo Publishing.

Printed in the United States of America, North Mankato, Minnesota
102017
012018

THIS BOOK CONTAINS
RECYCLED MATERIALS

Cover Photo: Vladimir Pesnya/Sputnik/AP Images
Interior Photos: Vladimir Pesnya/Sputnik/AP Images, 1; Kyodo/AP Images, 4–5; Ivan Sekretarev/ AP Images, 6, 34; Andrey Malgin/Shutterstock Images, 8–9; Sergey Nivens/Shutterstock Images, 10; Shutterstock Images, 12–13, 19, 31; Vincent Thian/AP Images, 15; Steven Senne/AP Images, 16 (left), 16 (right); Francois Mori/AP Images, 20–21; Kyodo/AP Images, 22; Jacques Demarthon/AFP/ Getty Images, 24–25; Goran Jakus/Shutterstock Images, 27; Conrad Huenich/ullstein bild/Getty Images, 28–29; Science & Society Picture Library/SSPL/Getty Images, 32 (top); Buyenlarge/Getty Images, 32 (middle); Steve Russell/Toronto Star/Getty Images, 32 (bottom); Ramil Sitdikov/Sputnik/ AP Images, 36–37; Petr David Josek/AP Images, 38–39; Iurii Osadchi/Shutterstock Images, 41; Kevork Djansezian/AP Images, 43 (top); Eric Gay/AP Images, 43 (middle), 43 (bottom); Olga Besnard/ Shutterstock Images, 45

Editor: Arnold Ringstad
Series Designer: Maggie Villaume
Content Consultant: Sarah Ridge, Assistant Professor, Exercise Sciences, Brigham Young University

PUBLISHER'S CATALOGING-IN-PUBLICATION DATA
Names: Ventura, Marne, author.
Title: STEM in figure skating / by Marne Ventura.
Description: Minneapolis, Minnesota : Abdo Publishing, 2018. | Series: STEM in sports | Includes online resources and index.
Identifiers: LCCN 2017946885 | ISBN 9781532113499 (lib.bdg.) | ISBN 9781532152375 (ebook)
Subjects: LCSH: Ice skating--Juvenile literature. | Sports sciences--Juvenile literature. | Physics--Juvenile literature.
Classification: DDC 796.91--dc23
LC record available at https://lccn.loc.gov/2017946885

The skating competitions at the Winter Olympics are among the most popular figure skating events in the world.

STEM ON ICE

Emma ran to the living room and turned on the television. The date was February 19, 2014. She settled onto the couch. Emma was following the Winter Olympics. Tonight was the Ladies' Short Program in Team Figure Skating. Figure skaters from 10 countries were at the Iceberg Skating Palace in Sochi, Russia. Each had 2 minutes and 50 seconds to complete a routine.

Ashley Wagner's skating skills earned her an Olympic medal.

Emma loved figure skating. After taking lessons, she could glide and stop on the ice. Her next goals were to spin and jump.

Now Emma watched as 22-year-old American skater Ashley Wagner entered the rink. The crowd in the stadium cheered and clapped as Wagner glided across the ice. She moved gracefully. This was possible because of low friction between the frozen water and the grooved blades of her skates. Wagner used her leg muscles to push her skates against the ice. She propelled herself into a triple flip, triple toe loop combination. Wagner followed this with a flying sit spin. She pulled her arms in close to increase her spin speed. Along with her US teammates, Wagner won a bronze medal at the Sochi Winter Olympics.

STEM IN ACTION

Olympic figure skaters are strong, graceful, and talented. They provide entertainment to fans around the world.

The sport also provides many examples of science, technology, engineering, and math (STEM) in action.

How is science important to figure skating? Every move a skater makes is subject to the laws of physics. Understanding physics concepts such as friction,

STEM concepts are at play in the graceful movements of pairs skaters.

motion, and momentum can help skaters perform their best. Science helps in other ways, too. New training techniques and good nutrition help athletes stay in top form.

Skaters of all ages combine strength, skill, and technology in their performances.

Technology has advanced in recent years. Instant video replay allows skaters and trainers to study their technique. Three-dimensional motion capture technology lets computer experts create models of figure skaters and experiment with different moves. The skaters can then use this feedback to improve their skills. Figure skating judges also use technology when they review performances.

Engineers have found many ways to create better figure skating gear and arenas. Boots and blades are designed to improve performance and protect skaters' legs and feet. New synthetic materials are used to make comfortable, safe costumes. Arenas with artificial ice are available year-round. Modern stadiums allow audiences to enjoy the show.

Math is also an important part of figure skating. Judges use numbers to decide the ranking of winners in competitions. Skaters work on routines that include the moves and jumps that will earn the most points. Geometry comes into play in the design of both rinks and skating routines. Skaters have to understand height, angles, and timing in order to create winning programs.

STEM plays a role in every component of figure skating, from a skater's practice sessions to Olympic gold medals. Advances in these fields have made big contributions to the sport. Science, technology, engineering, and math make modern figure skating work.

Whether a person is skating on a frozen pond or in an Olympic arena, the same key scientific concepts affect their motion.

2

SKATING SCIENCE

Physics is the science of matter, motion, and force. Understanding concepts such as friction, momentum, and the nature of ice helps athletes master strokes, jumps, spins, and landings. The latest information about physical fitness enables skaters to stay in top form.

ICE, FRICTION, AND MOMENTUM

Why is ice slippery? A thin layer of liquid water molecules covers ice. This top layer of water makes figure skating possible.

Imagine trying to skate across a concrete sidewalk. The skate blade wouldn't move because of the friction between the metal and the sidewalk. A blade gliding across ice meets with very little friction. This lets skaters move for long distances with a single push. To start, stop, gain speed, or change direction, skaters use friction to their advantage. They push the edge of the blade against the ice. This creates more friction. Controlling this friction with skill allows a skater to be agile on the ice.

Momentum is a description of an object's motion. It is equal to the object's mass times its velocity. The spin of an object is its angular momentum. When a skater is spinning, her angular momentum depends on how fast she's turning and the distribution of mass around her center. Once she starts spinning, she maintains most of her angular momentum. Some is lost due to friction between the skates and the ice. If she pulls her arms closer to her body, her distribution of mass changes.

Skaters skillfully apply friction to control their movements across the slick ice.

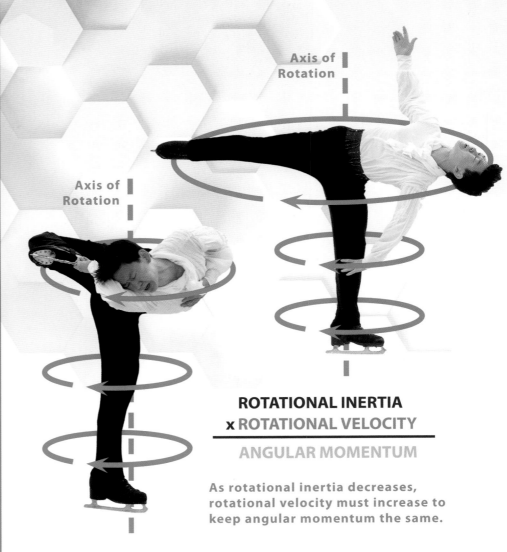

Axis of Rotation

Axis of Rotation

ROTATIONAL INERTIA
x ROTATIONAL VELOCITY
ANGULAR MOMENTUM

As rotational inertia decreases, rotational velocity must increase to keep angular momentum the same.

A spinning skater's axis of rotation is an imaginary line down through the center of his rotation. If no force besides gravity acts on a rotating object, such as in the air during a jump, its angular momentum will stay constant. When a skater begins rotating, he has angular momentum. His extended arms or legs are farthest from his axis of rotation and are moving quickly. Because angular momentum stays the same, when the skater pulls his leg closer to his body and reduces his rotational inertia, his spin speed increases to maintain the same momentum.

ANGULAR MOMENTUM

Her mass is less spread out around her rotational axis. This decreases her rotational inertia, which increases her spinning speed. When she extends her arms, the reverse happens. Her spin slows down.

Before a jump, a figure skater has linear momentum as he glides across the ice. To jump, he increases his speed and pushes against the ice with the toepick of

NEWTON'S LAWS OF MOTION

Sir Isaac Newton was an English scientist who lived from 1642 to 1727. His three laws of motion summarize some of the major properties of moving objects. The first law is that an object at rest stays at rest, and an object in motion stays in motion, until a force interferes. A skater will continue gliding until friction slows her down to a stop. The second law is that the more force is placed upon objects with the same mass, the greater the acceleration. The more force a skater uses to push herself into a jump, the more velocity the skater will have going into the air, and the higher the jump will be. Newton's third law is that for every action, there is an equal and opposite reaction. When a skater pushes her skate blades against the ice, the ice supplies a force that propels her into a glide.

his skate blade. This action transfers the force of his forward movement into upward, or vertical, momentum. The faster he is moving and the harder he pushes with his toe, the higher and longer his jump will be. At this point, angular momentum can be used to his advantage. Pulling in his arms will speed up any spinning motion he has. This allows him to spin more times in midair. The skater extends his arms and one leg to land on the ice.

THE SCIENCE OF TRAINING

Athletes need strength, endurance, and flexibility. To improve their performance, figure skaters practice on ice regularly. Repeated practice helps them master spins, jumps, starting, and stopping. Many skaters also practice ballet, Pilates, plyometrics, and yoga. Ballet promotes core strength and proper posture. Pilates is a form of exercise that increases flexibility and core strength. Plyometrics is a series of jumps, hops, and squats. The combination of stretching and contracting muscles builds strength, balance, and flexibility.

Practicing yoga between skating sessions can help figure skaters improve their flexibility.

Yoga poses strengthen the small muscles around hips, knees, and ankles that stabilize skaters. It also improves balance and coordination.

Smart figure skaters also follow modern nutritional advice. They eat plenty of fruits and vegetables, whole grains, and lean protein, and they stay hydrated with water. A smart diet and regular exercise will let them perform at their best.

Figure skating technology helps make dynamic, artistic performances possible.

CHAPTER **3**

FIGURE SKATING TECH

Technology is created when engineers use scientific information for practical purposes, such as building machines and equipment. Technology benefits figure skaters in many ways. Instant video replay helps skaters improve their routines. Three-dimensional computer modeling takes instant video replay to a new level. Judges of figure skating competitions also use video replay to evaluate performances.

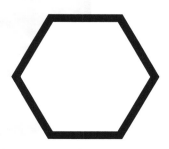

Imagine fanning the pages of a flip-book with the same image of a ball in a different position on each page. Flipping the pages quickly makes the ball appear to bounce like in a movie. Engineers reverse this process by creating a series of still images from a video recording. This technology allows viewers to see the individual movements that enabled the athlete to complete a jump.

VIDEO RECORDING AND COMPUTER ANALYSIS

Many coaches videotape skaters while they practice. Afterward, the skater and coach can watch the video in slow motion. This allows the skater to see which parts of his routine were done well and should be repeated, and where he needs to change for better performance. Athletes can also watch video recordings of top figure skaters and learn from their techniques.

Some coaches use computer software that analyzes the video recording and adds information to the video, such as the angle of the skater's axis of rotation during a spin. This technology lets viewers see exactly how a figure skater executes a move by showing a frame-by-frame still sequence of a jump or spin.

Jim Richards, a professor of biomechanics at the University of Delaware, is using technology to improve the performance of figure skaters in a new way. He goes a step beyond normal video recording by creating a video showing exactly what the skater should

have done. For example, when a skater fails to complete a jump because of incorrect posture, computer software creates a three-dimensional model of the skater that shows the correct posture and a successful jump.

This technology has helped skaters improve their

performance more quickly. Using trial and error with

a computer model reduces the risk that the skater will

injure himself while practicing a new move.

TECHNOLOGY FOR JUDGES

Instant video replay technology was used for the first time in Olympic figure skating at the 2002 Winter Games in Salt Lake City, Utah. Officials discovered unfair judging at these Olympics. They soon replaced the old scoring system with a more objective video replay system. With the new system, a technical specialist watches a video recording to identify and grade each

THE BENEFITS OF COMPUTER MODELING

Professor Richards's team at the University of Delaware creates computer models of figure skaters to help them find the air position they need for improving their jumps. After watching a skater's movements on a computer screen, the experts can manipulate the models to see what would happen if they changed some aspect of the skater's technique. To achieve more rotations during a jump, skaters need to spin faster in the air. By seeing what happens when the computer model increases speed to make a tough jump, skaters can learn the move with less risk of injury than by trial and error on the ice. Experts predict that one day this process will become widely available in the form of affordable, lightweight, portable sensors and a smartphone app.

Judges sit right alongside the ice to get the best possible view of performances.

skating element, such as foot position during takeoff or landing of a jump. Then, judges review the video and assign a final score.

The engineering behind figure skating has come a long way in the last century.

4

ENGINEERING A ROUTINE

An engineer is an expert in designing and building devices and structures. Over the years, engineers and innovative skaters have found many ways to make figure skating gear better. Boots, blades, clothing, and ice rinks have come a long way since the first skaters glided across frozen ponds wearing stiff suits and long skirts. Today, figure skating gear and ice rinks are better and safer than ever before.

BOOTS AND BLADES

The earliest skaters were simply looking for a way to move across frozen ponds. By the 1700s, people enjoyed skating as a fun pastime as well as a way to get around on ice. The first skating club was formed in Edinburgh, Scotland, in 1742. Jackson Haines, an American ballet dancer in the 1800s, is called the father of modern figure skating. He combined dance and music with ice skating.

EARLIEST ICE SKATES

Scientists studied skates found in Scandinavia and Russia from around 3000 BCE. The skates were made from animal bones. Holes were carved into the ends of the bones and leather straps were attached. These straps were used to secure the bone skates to shoes. According to historians, primitive skates were needed so people could cross frozen ice to hunt for food. The smooth bones didn't grip the ice, so early skaters used poles with sharpened ends to push themselves across the frozen water. While modern skaters can reach speeds of more than 35 miles per hour (56 km/h), bone skates probably moved at about 5 miles per hour (8 km/h).

Modern figure skate blades are designed to give skaters good control over their movement on the ice.

Today professional skaters wear custom-fitted leather boots. Thick padding covers and supports the ankle. A wide, cushioned tongue under a long row of laces gives better control, a snug fit, and flexibility.

Blades are made of slightly curved metal about 3/16 of an inch (4 mm) thick. A groove along the center of the blade creates an inside and outside edge, like an upside-down U. The front of the blade, called the

BONE SKATE, 1200s CE

ICE SKATE, 1880s

MODERN SKATE, 2013

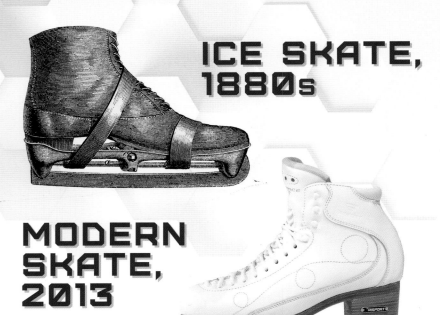

Since the first skaters moved across frozen ponds on animal bones, boot designers and inventive athletes have found many ways to improve upon the figure skate. During the 1300s, Dutch skaters attached iron bottom runners to their shoes with a leather strap. At this point, they still used poles to propel themselves. When a Dutch inventor added a metal double-edged blade around 1500, skaters could push and glide with their feet without the need for a pole. This was called the Dutch Roll. In 1865 American Jackson Haines developed blades that attached directly to boots and had toe picks, and modern toe-pick jumps were born.

toe pick, is serrated like a bread knife. This lets it generate friction against the ice. Skaters plant the toe pick into the ice to push off for jumps. Blades need to be sharpened regularly to work safely and properly.

Figure skaters getting ready to compete can practice as much as six or seven days a week for many years. During practice they might attempt 50 or 100 jumps each session. This puts a lot of stress on their bodies and can cause injuries that prevent them from competing. In 2014, researchers at Brigham Young University in Utah and Ithaca College in New York invented a device to measure the force of jumps. They created an ice skate with strain gauges attached to the blade. This smart skate might help figure skaters monitor their practice to prevent overuse injuries.

Attention-getting costumes are a fun part of today's competitive figure skating. The first figure skaters wore their normal street clothes on the ice. At the time, the style for women was full-length skirts. Sonja Henie was

Colorful costumes have become a familiar part of figure skating routines.

a Norwegian Olympic medalist in the 1920s and 1930s. She introduced the knee-length skirt for female skaters. Costumes got shorter as the years passed. In 1968, American figure skater Peggy Fleming wore tights and a hip-length skirt at the Winter Olympics in Grenoble, France. Clothing for male skaters evolved, too. Advances in fabric technology allowed for stretchy suits that enabled easier movement and a closer fit. Costumes with flair, such as rhinestone-studded leotards or theme costumes, became popular in the 1980s. In addition to making a fashion statement, modern costumes are designed to allow skaters to move more freely and avoid possible injury from loose clothing.

INDOOR ICE

The invention of refrigeration made it possible for figure skaters to practice their sport year-round. The Glaciarium in London, England, the first rink with artificially frozen ice, was built in 1876. In the United States, the first artificial ice rink was completed in

Madison Square Garden in New York City in 1879. Figure skating ice needs to be kept at a temperature between 26 and 28 degrees Fahrenheit (-3.3 to -2.2°C).

Olympic figure skating rink dimensions are 100 feet (30.5 m) by 200 feet (61 m). Having precise requirements

In 2017, authorities in Pyeongchang, South Korea, prepared their figure skating arena for the upcoming 2018 Winter Olympics.

for the engineering of ice rinks ensures that athletes from all over the world can know what to expect when they prepare for competition. From skates to costumes to artificial ice, engineering helps athletes stay safe and perform their best.

Skaters must take into account the size of the rink and precise timing when executing jumps and spins.

5

THE MATH OF FIGURE SKATING

Like science, technology, and engineering, math plays an important role in figure skating. Judges use a special number system to score athletes' performances. When skaters choreograph their moves, the geometry of the ice rink comes into play. Numbers are also important in the timing of figure skating routines.

Until 2002 judges used a scale from 0 to 6 to score performances at the Olympics. They rated how well the athletes completed moves such as jumps and spins. They also gave a score for presentation, including choreography, timing, and interpretation of music. At the 2002 Olympics, officials discovered that a judge voted unfairly. To make voting more objective, officials

2002 OLYMPIC SCORING SCANDAL

Figure skating at the 2002 Olympics featured a major controversy. During the pairs competition, Jamie Salé and David Pelletier of Canada were in second place behind Elena Berezhnaya and Anton Sikharulidze of Russia when they entered the free skate program. Berezhnaya and Sikharulidze made a small error during a double axel. Salé and Pelletier's routine was flawless. The crowd cheered wildly, and TV commentators predicted that the Canadians would receive high scores from the judges and win the gold medal. To everyone's surprise, the Russians outscored the Canadians. Officials confronted the French judge, who confessed that she made a deal to favor the Russians. Others argued that the Russians deserved to win. In the end, both teams were awarded the gold medal, and the judging system was revamped.

From spins on the ice to high-flying jumps, STEM principles can be found throughout the exciting sport of figure skating.

changed to a new system using a scale of 0 to 10. The new system was first used in 2004.

In the new system, two panels of officials judge the athletes. The technical panel is made up of five specialists. They video record the performance and identify the different moves in the routine. Each move has a preset base value. A more difficult jump has a higher value than a less difficult jump.

The technical panel passes their numbers to the nine-member judge panel. Each judge adds or subtracts up to 3 points based on how well the skater performed the move. A skater who performs perfectly might gain 3 points. If the skater falls, 3 points might be subtracted from the value of the move. This is the technical score.

The judges also give points on a scale from 0 to 10 for skating skill, transitions, performance, choreography, and interpretation. This is the presentation score. The final score is the sum of the technical and presentation scores.

TOE LOOP
(BASE VALUE: 0.4)

AXEL
(BASE VALUE: 0.8)

LUTZ
(BASE VALUE: 0.6)

Six kinds of jumps are counted as elements in International Skating Union competitions. Skaters either push off from the ice with the edges of their skate blades or with their toe picks. The Salchow, loop, and axel are edge jumps. The toe loop, flip, and Lutz are toe jumps. The axel is the most difficult because it includes an extra half rotation.

All of this number crunching is important for competitive skaters to understand when planning routines. Trying more difficult moves can earn them higher base scores. But if they make an error on those moves, they could lose points instead. Skaters must balance risk, reward, and their confidence when planning out the math of a winning routine.

MORE NUMBERS

The geometry of the ice rink and the timing of routines are two more areas where math is used in figure skating. Ice rinks are rectangular, but the corners are rounded so that skaters can more easily turn. Choreographers design routines that include a variety of moves. Some are parallel to the long axis, and some are parallel to the short axis of the rink. Diagonal moves are also included to make routines more interesting. A good figure skating routine will take advantage of the entire rink and avoid staying in a single area for too long.

Coordination and timing are especially important for pairs skaters.

Timing is important for athletes, too. When figure skaters push off of the ice for jumps they need to propel themselves high enough to do the correct number of rotations. Mistiming can cause the skater to fall or even hit the wall.

Figure skating has come a long way since the earliest skaters strapped bones onto their shoes. From the physics of a spin to the video recording of a jump, and from modern costumes and skating rinks to fair scoring, STEM continues to make figure skating a popular sport for athletes and audiences alike.

GLOSSARY

ACCELERATION
A change in speed or direction.

CHOREOGRAPHER
An expert at creating dance routines.

FORCE
A push or pull by one object on another object.

FRICTION
A force that resists motion between two objects that are touching.

LINEAR
In a straight line.

MASS
The amount of matter that makes up an object.

MOLECULE
A particle made up of atoms that forms the most basic element of a substance.

NUTRITION
The process by which people use food for energy.

PHYSICS
The branch of science that deals with matter and energy and how they interact.

VERTICAL
Going straight up or down.

ONLINE RESOURCES

To learn more about STEM in figure skating, visit **abdobooklinks.com**. These links are routinely monitored and updated to provide the most current information available.

MORE INFORMATION

BOOKS

Barnas, Jo-Ann. *Great Moments in Olympic Skating.* Minneapolis, MN: Abdo Publishing, 2015.

MacKay, Jenny. *Figure Skating.* Detroit, MI: Lucent Books, 2012.

Slingerland, Janet. *Sports Science and Technology in the Real World.* Minneapolis, MN: Abdo Publishing, 2017.

INDEX

ABOUT THE AUTHOR

Marne Ventura is the author of many books for kids, both fiction and nonfiction. She enjoys writing about science, technology, engineering, and math, arts and crafts, and the lives of creative people. A former elementary school teacher, Marne holds a master's degree in education from the University of California. She and her husband live on the central coast of California.